SHAPES THAT ROLL

KAREN NAGEL

SHAPES THAT

ISBN 978-0-545-30874-8

Text copyright © 2009 by Karen Nagel. Illustrations copyright © 2009 by Steve Wilson. All rights reserved. Published by Scholastic Inc., 557 Broadway, New York, NY 10012, by arrangement with Blue Apple Books, c/o Chronicle Books. SCHOLASTIC and associated logos are trademarks and/or registered trademarks of Scholastic Inc.

12 11 10 9 8 7 6 5 4   12 13 14 15/0

Printed in the U.S.A.

First Scholastic printing, October 2010

ROLL

illustrations by
STEVE WILSON

SCHOLASTIC INC.
New York Toronto London Auckland
Sydney Mexico City New Delhi Hong Kong

and **SQUARE**.

CIRCLE,

Follow the

TRIANGLE,

Follow them **HERE**.

Follow them **THERE**.

Follow them **HIGH**.

Follow them **LOW**.

UP and **DOWN** to the places they'll go.

They'll
show you
shapes
that **SLANT**, **STACK**, and **ROLL**.

Shapes that are **HALF**, shapes that are **WHOLE**.

Shapes that are **ROUND**

Shapes with **8 SIDES**.

Let these
three different shapes
be your expert shape guides.

Shapes that ROLL

Shapes that CAN'T

Shapes
with
sides
that
angle
and
SLANT.

Some shapes **STACK**

Some shapes **DON'T**

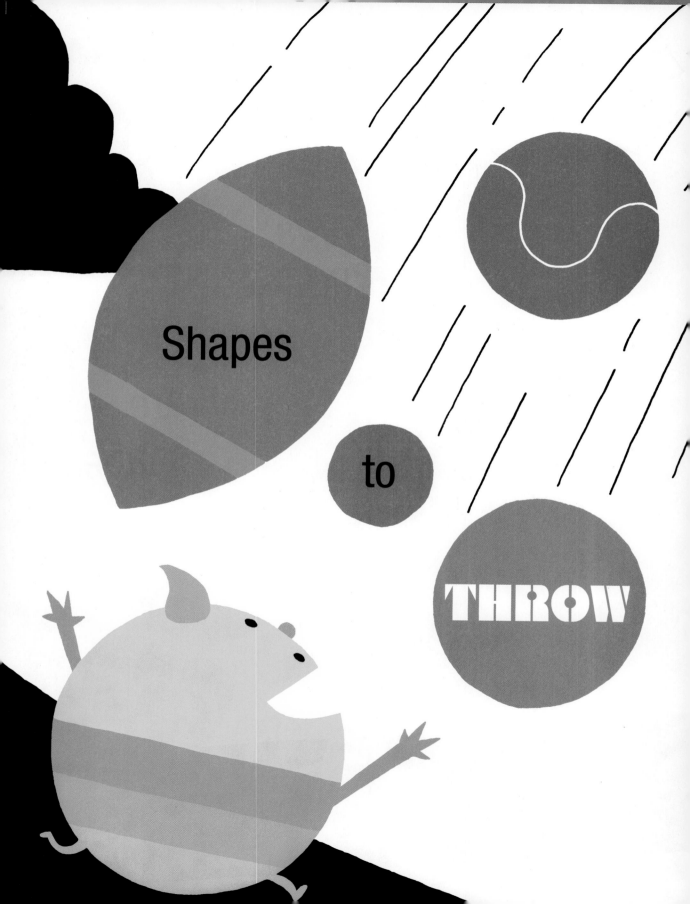

Shapes to **THROW**

Shapes to
SHARE

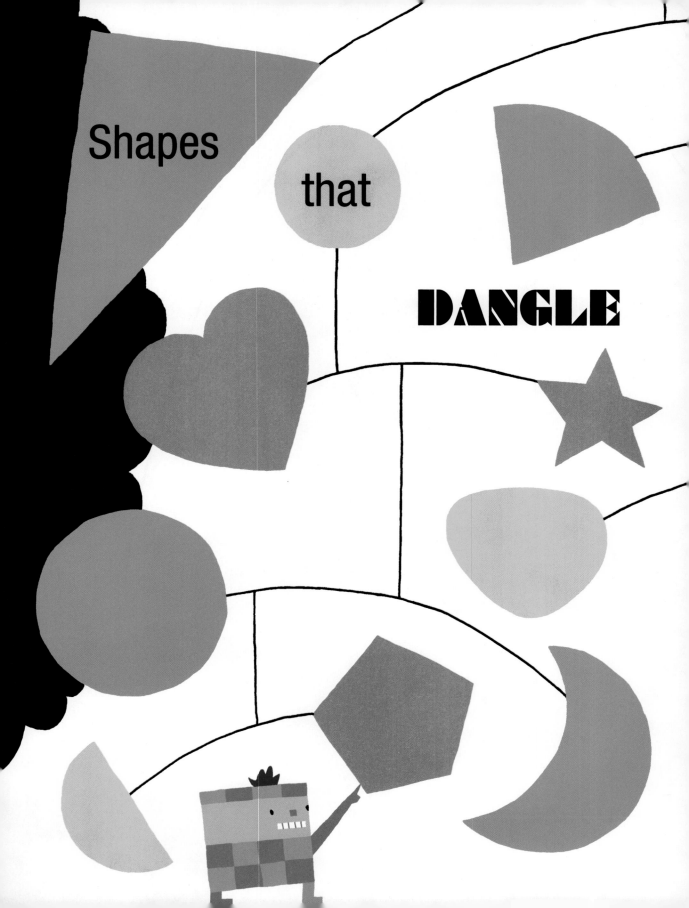

Shapes that DANGLE

in

the

AIR.

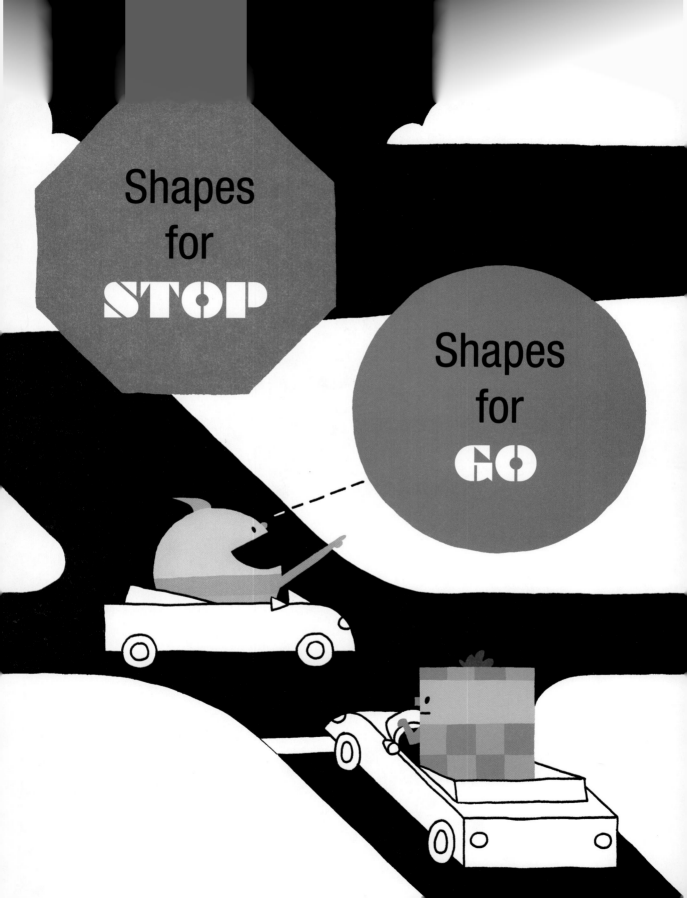

A house

has
many
shapes

to **SHOW**.

Shapes that SHINE

Shapes that FREEZE

Shapes
that
glimmer
up
ABOVE

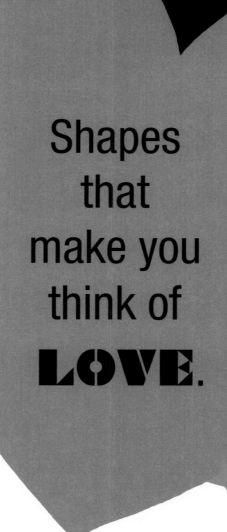

Shapes
that
make you
think of
LOVE.

Shapes to **OPEN**

Shapes to **CLOSE**

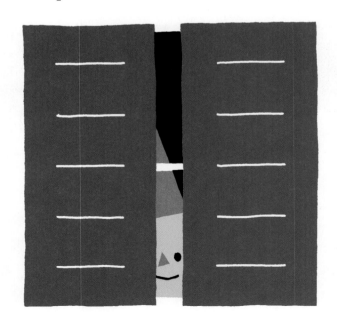

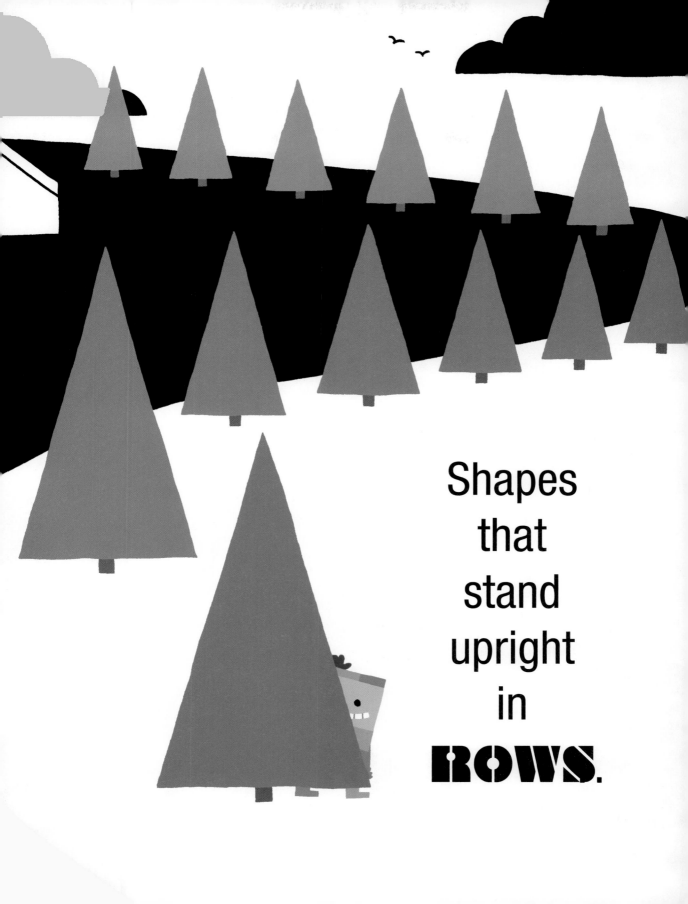

Shapes
that
stand
upright
in
ROWS.

Shapes that
TEETER

Shapes that
PLAY

Shapes
help
people
find their
WAY.

A shape that's
WHOLE

A shape in **PIECES**

Shapes
with many folds and
CREASES.

Shapes
are
HEAVY

Shapes are
LIGHT

Pillow shapes
are sure to
FIGHT.

Spheres are
ROUND

Circles are
FLAT

Squares **LIE DOWN**

Did you see the arrows,

the circles,

and the squares?

Did you see the stars,

and hearts,

and ovals everywhere?

Triangles,

rectangles,

diamonds,

pentagons of blue.

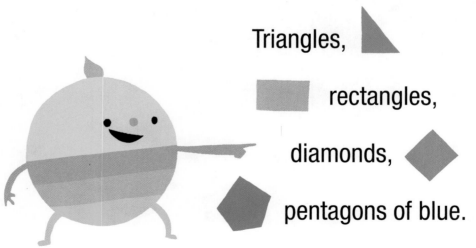

Crescents,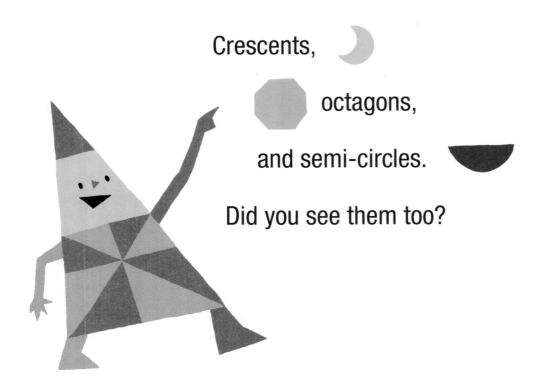

octagons,

and semi-circles.

Did you see them too?

SHAPES

of every size and kind

are found inside this book.

The whole wide world

is made of shapes. . .

they're
EVERYWHERE
you look!